Effective Strategies for Coping with Anxiety Disorders

The complete guide to overcoming anxiety attacks and maintaining a balance mental health

Henry H. Welch

Copyright

Disclaimer

The information provided in this book is for educational and informational purposes only. It is not a substitute for professional advice or treatment. While every effort has been made to ensure the accuracy of the information presented, the author and publisher make no representations or warranties of any kind, express or implied, about the completeness, accuracy, reliability, suitability, or availability concerning the content contained herein.

Readers are advised to consult with qualified healthcare professionals, therapists, or counselors for specific advice related to their individual circumstances. The author and publisher disclaim any liability for any loss, injury, or damage incurred as a direct or indirect consequence of the use and application of any content provided in this book.

Table of contents

Introduction

The importance of understanding anxiety disorders

In our rapidly evolving world, where daily pressures and challenges are a constant presence, it is of paramount importance to delve into the intricate realm of anxiety disorders. These disorders affect millions of individuals and extend far beyond the scope of transient moments of worry or fear that we all experience from time to time.

Anxiety disorders are not mere fleeting discomforts; they are pervasive conditions that can profoundly impact an individual's capacity to function in their daily life. From Generalized Anxiety Disorder (GAD) and Social Anxiety Disorder to Panic Disorder, these conditions cast a long shadow over mental and physical well-being.

Why is it crucial to understand anxiety disorders? The answer lies in the collective well-being of society. By comprehending the intricacies of anxiety disorders, we empower ourselves and those we hold dear to navigate these formidable challenges more effectively. This book embarks on a journey into the heart of anxiety, illuminating the causes, symptoms, diagnosis, and most importantly, the coping strategies that provide a lifeline.

As we embark on this exploration, we will uncover the various forms of anxiety disorders, the intricate web of their causative factors, the distinctive imprints they leave on the lives they touch, and the treatment options that offer hope. We will delve into coping strategies that not only help manage anxiety in day-to-day life but also prove invaluable during the recovery process.

By attaining a profound understanding of anxiety disorders, we open doors to empathy, support, and ultimately, a brighter future for ourselves and our loved ones. Join me on this journey as we navigate the labyrinthine landscape of anxiety disorders and embark on the path to healing and thriving.

Chapter 1: Unveiling Anxiety

Anxiety disorders and their significance

Anxiety disorders encompass a broad spectrum of mental health conditions characterized by excessive fear, worry, and physical symptoms that can significantly impact an individual's daily life and overall well-being. While it's normal for people to experience occasional anxiety or fear in response to life's challenges, anxiety disorders are more than just momentary discomfort. They represent persistent and often overwhelming states of unease that can disrupt daily activities, impair job performance, hinder relationships, and create a heavy burden on those affected.

The Significance of Understanding Anxiety Disorders

Understanding anxiety disorders is of paramount significance in today's society. Here are some key reasons why:

Prevalence: Anxiety disorders are far from rare. In the United States alone, around 40 million people grapple with anxiety disorders, making it one of the most common mental health conditions. By comprehending these disorders, we can better appreciate the widespread impact they have on individuals, families, and communities.

Quality of Life: Anxiety disorders are not limited to moments of discomfort. They can be all-consuming, affecting an individual's ability to function effectively. By understanding the significance of these disorders, we can empathize with the daily challenges faced by those who experience them and strive to improve their quality of life.

Early Intervention: Recognizing the signs of anxiety disorders and their significance allows for early intervention and timely treatment. The sooner anxiety disorders are diagnosed and addressed, the better the outcomes for individuals seeking to regain control of their lives.

Stigma Reduction: A comprehensive understanding of anxiety disorders can help reduce the stigma surrounding mental health issues. By fostering empathy and compassion, we create a more supportive environment for individuals to seek help and support.

Support: Knowing how to support someone with an anxiety disorder is crucial. Whether it's a friend, family member, or colleague, understanding the significance of anxiety disorders enables us to provide the necessary support and encouragement for their recovery journey.

As we delve deeper into this book, we will explore the various types of anxiety disorders, their causes, symptoms, diagnosis, treatment, and coping strategies. By shedding light on these important aspects, we aim to empower individuals to navigate the challenges of anxiety disorders, leading to a brighter, more empathetic, and supportive future for all.

Highlight the prevalence of anxiety disorders in the U.S

Anxiety disorders are not isolated conditions affecting only a small portion of the population; they have a significant and widespread presence in the United States. Understanding the prevalence of these disorders is vital for grasping the magnitude of their impact on society.

In the U.S., anxiety disorders are alarmingly common, with millions of individuals grappling with their effects. As of recent data, it is estimated that approximately 40 million people in the United States are affected by anxiety disorders. This staggering number represents a substantial portion of the population, making anxiety disorders one of the most prevalent mental health conditions in the country.

This high prevalence extends across various age groups, demographics, and regions. It affects men and women, young and old, people from all walks of life. The ubiquity of anxiety disorders emphasizes the need for a comprehensive understanding of these conditions, not only among healthcare professionals but also within the broader community.

As we delve deeper into this book, we will explore the different forms of anxiety disorders, their causes, symptoms, diagnosis, and treatment options. By gaining insight into these aspects, we hope to foster greater awareness and empathy, reducing the stigma surrounding anxiety disorders and providing support to the millions of individuals who are on their journey to cope, heal, and thrive.

Chapter 2: Types of Anxiety Disorders

Exploring common anxiety disorders

Anxiety disorders are diverse and can manifest in various ways, affecting individuals differently. In this chapter, we will delve into three of the most prevalent anxiety disorders: Generalized Anxiety Disorder (GAD), Social Anxiety Disorder, and Panic Disorder. Understanding these distinct disorders is essential for recognizing their symptoms and offering appropriate support and treatment.

Generalized Anxiety Disorder (GAD)

Generalized Anxiety Disorder, often abbreviated as GAD, is a widespread anxiety disorder characterized by persistent and excessive worry about everyday matters. Individuals with GAD experience ongoing anxiety that can extend beyond specific triggers. They may worry about a range of issues, including job duties, family health, daily chores, car repairs, and appointments. The worry is often disproportionate to the situation and can significantly impact an individual's quality of life.

Symptoms of GAD may include restlessness, feeling on edge or easily fatigued, difficulty concentrating, muscle tension, and difficulties with sleeping. Managing GAD typically involves various treatment approaches, including cognitive-behavioral therapy, medication, and lifestyle changes.

Social Anxiety Disorder

Social Anxiety Disorder, also known as social phobia, is another common anxiety disorder that revolves around the fear of social situations. People with social anxiety disorder often experience extreme anxiety when faced with social interactions. This can include the fear of public speaking, introducing oneself to new people, or even eating or drinking in public. Such situations can trigger intense anxiety, avoidance, and physical symptoms like rapid heartbeat and sweating.

Panic Disorder

Panic Disorder is marked by sudden and intense panic attacks. These attacks can be terrifying, often resembling symptoms of heart attacks. During a panic attack, individuals may experience a rapid heartbeat, difficulty catching their breath, dizziness, and other distressing symptoms. Panic attacks can occur alongside other anxiety disorders and often begin between the ages of 20-24.

Understanding these common anxiety disorders is the first step in offering support and guidance to individuals who may be affected by them. In the chapters that follow, we will delve deeper into the causes, symptoms, diagnosis, and treatment options for each of these disorders, providing a comprehensive view of how they impact lives and how they can be effectively managed.

Discuss symptoms and specific characteristics of each disorder

Understanding anxiety disorders involves not only recognizing the various types but also comprehending the specific symptoms and characteristics that define each disorder. In this section, we will delve into the symptoms and unique attributes of three common anxiety disorders: Generalized

Anxiety Disorder (GAD), Social Anxiety Disorder, and Panic Disorder.

Generalized Anxiety Disorder (GAD)

Symptoms

Persistent Worry: Individuals with GAD experience relentless and excessive worry about everyday matters, often with no apparent reason. Their concerns extend to various aspects of life, such as family, work, health, and daily tasks.

Physical Symptoms: GAD is not limited to mental distress; it often manifests in physical symptoms. Common physical indicators include muscle tension, restlessness, feeling on edge, and excessive fatigue.

Difficulty Concentrating: The constant state of worry can make it challenging to concentrate or focus on tasks, leading to decreased productivity and efficiency.

Sleep Disturbances: Individuals with GAD may struggle with sleep, experiencing difficulties falling asleep or staying asleep.

Specific Characteristics

Chronic Nature: GAD is characterized by its chronic and persistent nature. It often lasts for months or even years, with individuals experiencing symptoms on most days.

Worry Proportions: The worry experienced in GAD is often disproportionate to the actual situations or issues, leading to significant distress.

Social Anxiety Disorder

Symptoms

Extreme Social Fear: Social Anxiety Disorder is marked by an intense fear of social situations. Individuals may dread activities like public speaking, meeting new people, or even eating in public.

Avoidance Behavior: To cope with their fear, individuals with social anxiety often engage in avoidance behavior, sidestepping social situations that trigger anxiety.

Physical Symptoms: Social anxiety can lead to physical symptoms, including sweating, trembling, a racing heart, and blushing when facing social interactions.

Specific Characteristics

Focus on Social Evaluation: People with social anxiety tend to focus on how they are perceived by others, often fearing judgment or embarrassment.

Interferes with Daily Life: Social Anxiety Disorder can hinder a person's ability to pursue relationships, education, and employment due to the overwhelming fear of social interactions.

Panic Disorder

Symptoms:

Sudden Panic Attacks: Panic Disorder is characterized by recurrent and unexpected panic attacks. These attacks involve a rapid and intense onset of fear and physical symptoms such as a racing heart, shortness of breath, and dizziness.
Fear of Panic Attacks: Individuals with Panic Disorder often develop a fear of future panic attacks, leading to a cycle of anxiety and avoidance.

Specific Characteristics

Misinterpretation of Physical Symptoms: Panic attacks are often triggered by a misinterpretation of bodily sensations as life-threatening, contributing to the fear and intensity of the attacks.
Overlap with Other Anxiety Disorders: Panic Disorder can co-occur

with other anxiety disorders, compounding the overall anxiety burden.

Understanding the specific symptoms and characteristics of these anxiety disorders is crucial for early recognition and effective intervention. In the following chapters, we will explore the causes, diagnosis, and treatment options for each disorder, offering a comprehensive view of how to manage and support individuals affected by these conditions.

Chapter 3: The Complex Causes

Investigate the multifaceted causes of anxiety disorders

Anxiety disorders are complex conditions with multifaceted causes that arise from a combination of genetic, environmental, and psychological factors. Understanding these causes is essential for gaining insight into the origins of anxiety disorders and paving the way for effective treatment and support.

Genetic Factors

One prominent aspect of anxiety disorders is their genetic component. Research has shown that anxiety disorders can run in families, suggesting a genetic predisposition to these conditions. There is evidence of common genetic factors linking Generalized Anxiety Disorder (GAD) to other internalizing disorders. These genetic factors can make some individuals more vulnerable to developing an anxiety disorder if there is a family history of such conditions.

Environmental Factors

Anxiety disorders can also be influenced by environmental factors. Traumatic life events, ongoing stress, and underlying medical conditions can contribute to the development of these disorders. Negative parenting practices, life events such as loss or trauma, and overall life circumstances can also play a role in the onset of anxiety disorders.

Psychological Factors

Psychological factors, including cognitive patterns and coping strategies, can impact the development and exacerbation of anxiety disorders. For example, individuals with a tendency to catastrophize situations or overanalyze their experiences may be at a higher risk of developing anxiety disorders.

Risk Factors

Several risk factors can increase an individual's susceptibility to anxiety disorders. Gender plays a role, as women tend to experience hormonal fluctuations that may contribute to anxiety, while men have higher levels of testosterone, which might offer some protection against anxiety. This gender difference suggests that hormonal variations can influence anxiety levels.

It's important to recognize that anxiety disorders often have a multifactorial cause, with various factors interacting and contributing to the development of these conditions. As we explore this complex interplay in the following chapters, we aim to shed light on how these causes influence the symptoms, diagnosis, and treatment of anxiety disorders. This understanding is crucial for providing comprehensive support and effective intervention to those affected by anxiety disorders.

Discuss genetic, environmental, and psychological factors

To unravel the intricate tapestry of anxiety disorders, we must examine the three foundational pillars upon which they rest: genetic, environmental, and psychological factors. Each plays a pivotal role in the development and exacerbation of these conditions, painting a multifaceted picture of their origins.

Genetic Factors

Genetic Predisposition: Genetic factors are a significant influence on the development of anxiety disorders. It's not uncommon to find a family history of anxiety disorders, suggesting a genetic predisposition. Studies have indicated that specific genetic factors are shared among individuals with Generalized Anxiety Disorder (GAD) and other internalizing disorders. This genetic link serves as a vital clue in understanding the hereditary nature of anxiety disorders.

Inherited Vulnerability: Genetics can make certain individuals more vulnerable to anxiety disorders if there is a familial history of such conditions. This inherited vulnerability underscores the role of genes in shaping an individual's susceptibility to anxiety disorders.

Environmental Factors

Traumatic Life Events: Environmental factors play a substantial role in the onset of anxiety disorders. Traumatic life events, such as accidents, loss, or abuse, can be potent triggers. These experiences may serve as catalysts for the development of anxiety disorders, emphasizing the importance of early intervention and support for individuals who have experienced trauma.

Chronic Stress: Ongoing stress can act as a precursor to anxiety disorders. The relentless pressure of modern life, including work-related stress and social pressures, can erode an individual's resilience and contribute to the emergence of anxiety.

Parenting Practices: Negative parenting practices can also be a contributing environmental factor. The way individuals are raised and the parenting styles they experience can have a lasting impact on their psychological well-being, potentially increasing the risk of anxiety disorders.

Psychological Factors

Cognitive Patterns: Psychological factors, including cognitive patterns and coping strategies, play a pivotal role in anxiety disorders. Individuals who tend to catastrophize situations or engage in constant overanalysis are more susceptible to developing anxiety disorders. These cognitive patterns can influence how individuals perceive and respond to stressful situations.

Personality Traits: Certain personality traits, such as perfectionism and a predisposition to excessive worry, can make individuals more prone to anxiety disorders. Anxious individuals may have a heightened sensitivity to perceived threats and a lower tolerance for uncertainty.

Understanding the interplay of these genetic, environmental, and psychological factors is crucial in unraveling the causes of anxiety disorders. By shedding light on these complex origins, we can better comprehend how these conditions manifest and, in turn, develop more effective strategies for their management and treatment. In the subsequent chapters, we will explore how these factors influence the symptoms, diagnosis, and treatment of anxiety disorders.

Chapter 4: Recognizing the Symptoms

Detail the physical and mental symptoms of anxiety disorders

Recognizing anxiety disorders begins with a keen awareness of the diverse symptoms that manifest in both physical and mental dimensions. These symptoms can vary depending on the specific anxiety disorder, but they share common threads that reveal the underlying distress experienced by those affected.

Physical Symptoms

Rapid Heartbeat: One of the hallmark physical symptoms of anxiety disorders is an increased heart rate. This rapid heartbeat is a physiological response to the body's "fight or flight" reaction to stress.

Shortness of Breath: Anxiety can lead to shallow, rapid breathing or a feeling of breathlessness. Individuals may struggle to catch their breath during anxiety episodes.

Dizziness: Many people with anxiety disorders report feeling lightheaded or dizzy during episodes of anxiety. This can contribute to a sense of unsteadiness and discomfort.

Muscle Tension: Anxiety often leads to muscle tension and physical discomfort. Individuals may experience muscle stiffness, especially in the neck, shoulders, and back.

Gastrointestinal Distress: Anxiety can manifest in digestive issues, including nausea, stomachaches, and changes in bowel habits.

Sweating: Excessive sweating is a common physical symptom of anxiety. It can lead to profuse sweating, especially in stressful social situations.

Trembling: Individuals may experience trembling or shaking in response to anxiety. This physical symptom can be quite noticeable and can contribute to feelings of embarrassment.

Headaches: Anxiety can trigger tension headaches or migraines. These headaches can be intense and debilitating.

Mental Symptoms

Excessive Worry: A hallmark mental symptom of anxiety disorders is excessive, intrusive worry. Individuals may find it difficult to control their worrying, and these thoughts can be irrational or out of proportion to the situation.

Intense Fear: Anxiety often involves an intense sense of fear or apprehension. This fear can be triggered by specific situations or may arise without an apparent cause.

Impending Doom: People with anxiety disorders may experience a pervasive sense of impending doom or a feeling that something terrible is about to happen.

Inability to Concentrate: Anxiety can make it challenging to concentrate or focus on tasks. This mental symptom can lead to decreased productivity and efficiency.

Irritability: Individuals with anxiety disorders may become easily irritated or agitated. This emotional response is often related to the ongoing distress caused by anxiety.

Panic Attacks: In panic disorders, panic attacks are a specific mental symptom. These episodes involve sudden and intense fear, often accompanied by physical symptoms such as a racing heart and shortness of breath.

Recognizing the intricate interplay of physical and mental symptoms is crucial for the early identification and understanding of anxiety disorders. In the following chapters, we will explore the diagnostic process and various treatment options that target these symptoms, providing individuals with the support and guidance they need to navigate the challenges of anxiety disorders.

Explain the "fight or flight" response and its impact

The "fight or flight" response is a fundamental physiological reaction that occurs in response to stress or perceived threats. This response, also known as the acute stress response, triggers a series of physiological and psychological changes designed to prepare the body to confront or escape from a perceived danger. While this response can be lifesaving in genuine life-threatening situations, it plays a central role in the symptoms of anxiety disorders.

The "Fight or Flight" Response

When the brain perceives a threat or stressful situation, it sends signals to the body to prepare for action. This process involves the release of stress hormones, primarily adrenaline and cortisol, which initiate a cascade of changes in the body:

Increased Heart Rate: One of the immediate effects of the "fight or flight" response is an elevated heart rate. This serves to pump more blood to the muscles and vital organs, preparing the body for action.

Rapid Breathing: Breathing becomes faster and more shallow, increasing the oxygen supply to the bloodstream. This heightened oxygen level is essential for increased physical exertion.

Muscle Tension: Muscles tighten and become more rigid, preparing for swift movement or action.

Dilated Pupils: The pupils of the eyes dilate, allowing more light to enter. This improves vision in low-light conditions or situations where acute visual perception is required.

Blood Sugar Elevation: The liver releases glucose into the bloodstream, providing an immediate energy source for the body's heightened demands.

Sweating: The body begins to sweat to cool itself down during physical exertion, which often accompanies the "fight or flight" response.

Digestive Inhibition: Digestive processes slow down or temporarily halt to redirect energy and resources to more immediate survival needs.

Impact on Anxiety Disorders

In individuals with anxiety disorders, the "fight or flight" response can be triggered inappropriately or excessively in situations that are not genuinely life-threatening. This hyperactivation of the stress response can lead to a range of physical and mental symptoms characteristic of anxiety disorders, such as rapid heartbeat, shortness of breath, muscle tension, excessive worry, and fear.

Understanding the impact of the "fight or flight" response on anxiety disorders is essential for both individuals experiencing these conditions and those providing support and treatment. In the following chapters, we will explore how to manage and mitigate the effects of this response and its role in the symptoms of anxiety disorders.

Chapter 5: Diagnosis and Assessment

The process of diagnosing anxiety disorders

Diagnosing anxiety disorders is a complex and multi-faceted process that involves a comprehensive evaluation of an individual's symptoms, medical history, and psychological state. The goal is to accurately identify the specific anxiety disorder and its severity, enabling healthcare professionals to develop an effective treatment plan.

Diagnostic Criteria

Anxiety disorders are diagnosed based on specific criteria outlined in the Diagnostic and Statistical Manual of Mental Disorders (DSM-5), published by the American Psychiatric Association. This manual provides a standardized framework for mental health professionals to make consistent and accurate diagnoses. To diagnose an anxiety disorder, the following criteria must be met:

Presence of Symptoms: The individual must exhibit a range of symptoms consistent with the specific anxiety disorder. These symptoms may include excessive worry, fear, and physical manifestations such as rapid heartbeat and muscle tension.

Duration and Severity: The symptoms must persist for a certain duration and reach a particular level of severity to meet the diagnostic criteria.

The Diagnostic Process

Clinical Interview: The first step in diagnosing an anxiety disorder is a clinical interview with a mental health professional. During this interview, the individual provides a detailed history of their symptoms, including their duration and impact on daily life.

Medical History: The mental health professional may inquire about the individual's medical history, including any family history of anxiety disorders or other mental health conditions. This information helps in understanding potential genetic factors.

Physical Exam: A physical examination may be conducted to rule out any underlying medical conditions that could be contributing to the symptoms. Certain medical conditions can mimic the symptoms of anxiety disorders.

Psychological Evaluation: The mental health professional may perform psychological assessments or questionnaires to further evaluate the individual's mental state and the specific anxiety disorder.

Differential Diagnosis: Anxiety symptoms can overlap with other mental health conditions, such as depression or post-traumatic stress disorder. A differential diagnosis helps distinguish anxiety disorders from other disorders with similar symptoms.

Severity Assessment

The assessment of severity is crucial in determining the appropriate treatment approach. Anxiety disorders can range from mild to severe, and treatment plans are tailored to the individual's level of distress and impairment in daily life.

Diagnosing anxiety disorders is a meticulous process that requires the expertise of trained mental health professionals. A precise diagnosis is the cornerstone of effective treatment, as it guides the selection of therapeutic interventions and support strategies. In the following chapters, we will delve into the various treatment options available for managing anxiety disorders based on the diagnosis and severity of the condition.

The importance of medical history, physical exams, and psychological evaluations

Diagnosing anxiety disorders is a nuanced process that relies on a comprehensive evaluation of an individual's symptoms and overall health. Key components of this evaluation include obtaining a thorough medical history, conducting physical exams, and performing psychological assessments. The importance of each of these components cannot be overstated.

Medical History

Identifying Risk Factors: A detailed medical history can reveal potential risk factors for anxiety disorders, such as a family history of mental health conditions. Understanding these risk factors is essential for a more accurate diagnosis and tailored treatment plan.

Rule Out Medical Causes: Certain medical conditions, such as thyroid disorders or cardiovascular issues, can present symptoms that mimic those of anxiety disorders. A comprehensive medical history helps in identifying and ruling out these potential underlying causes.

Medication and Substance Use: Information about previous and current medications, as well as substance use, is critical. Some medications and substances can contribute to or exacerbate anxiety symptoms.

Physical Exams

Ruling Out Medical Conditions: Physical examinations are valuable in ruling out physical health conditions that may be contributing to anxiety symptoms. For example, an overactive thyroid or heart condition can cause symptoms like rapid heartbeat and restlessness.

Detecting Subtle Signs: A physical exam can detect subtle physical signs of anxiety, such as muscle tension and changes in blood pressure. These physical manifestations provide additional clues for diagnosis.

Overall Health Assessment: A physical exam offers a holistic assessment of the individual's overall health. This information helps in creating a complete clinical picture and guiding treatment decisions.

Psychological Evaluations

Assessing Mental State: Psychological evaluations involve assessing the individual's mental state, including their emotional well-being and thought processes. These evaluations help in understanding the emotional and cognitive aspects of anxiety.

Identification of Specific Disorder: Different anxiety disorders can have unique psychological markers. A psychological evaluation aids in pinpointing the specific disorder, such as Generalized Anxiety Disorder (GAD) or Social Anxiety Disorder.

Severity Assessment**: Psychological assessments help in gauging the severity of anxiety symptoms and their impact on daily life. This assessment is crucial for treatment planning.

Differential Diagnosis: Psychological evaluations assist in distinguishing anxiety disorders from other mental health conditions with similar symptoms, such as depression or post-traumatic stress disorder. Accurate differentiation is essential for tailored treatment.

The combination of medical history, physical exams, and psychological evaluations provides a comprehensive view of the individual's condition. It helps mental health professionals in making accurate diagnoses and developing personalized treatment plans. By understanding the individual's medical and psychological background, healthcare providers can offer more effective support and intervention. In the following chapters, we will explore various treatment options and strategies based on the diagnosis and severity of the anxiety disorder.

Chapter 6: Treatment Approaches

Various treatment options, including psychotherapy and medication

Effective treatment for anxiety disorders encompasses a range of therapeutic approaches, each designed to address the unique needs and circumstances of individuals affected by these conditions. Among the primary treatment options are psychotherapy and medication.

Psychotherapy

Psychotherapy, often referred to as talk therapy, is a cornerstone of anxiety disorder treatment. It involves working with a mental health professional to address the emotional and psychological aspects of anxiety. There are several types of psychotherapy commonly used to manage anxiety disorders:

Cognitive-Behavioral Therapy (CBT): CBT is one of the most widely utilized therapeutic approaches for anxiety disorders. It focuses on identifying and modifying irrational thought patterns and behaviors that contribute to anxiety. CBT equips individuals with practical skills to manage anxiety effectively.

Exposure Therapy: This form of therapy is particularly effective for specific phobias and certain anxiety disorders. It involves gradually exposing individuals to their feared situations or objects, helping them desensitize and learn to manage their fear response.

Dialectical Behavior Therapy (DBT): DBT is beneficial for individuals with anxiety disorders who also struggle with emotional regulation. It teaches mindfulness and coping skills to manage intense emotions.

Interpersonal Therapy (IPT): IPT is focused on improving interpersonal relationships and communication. It can be helpful for individuals with social anxiety disorder or generalized anxiety disorder who experience difficulties in social interactions.

Medication

Medications can be a valuable adjunct to psychotherapy, particularly for individuals with moderate to severe anxiety disorders. Some commonly prescribed medications for anxiety disorders include:

Selective Serotonin Reuptake Inhibitors (SSRIs): SSRIs are a type of antidepressant often used to treat anxiety disorders. They work by increasing the availability of serotonin in the brain, which can help improve mood and reduce anxiety.

Benzodiazepines: These medications are used for short-term relief of severe anxiety symptoms, as they can be habit-forming. They work by enhancing the effects of a neurotransmitter called gamma-aminobutyric acid (GABA), which has a calming effect on the brain.

Serotonin-Norepinephrine Reuptake Inhibitors (SNRIs): SNRIs are another class of antidepressants that can be effective in treating anxiety disorders. They work by increasing the availability of both serotonin and norepinephrine in the brain.

Beta-Blockers: Beta-blockers are often prescribed for individuals with social anxiety disorder to manage physical symptoms of anxiety, such as rapid heartbeat and trembling.

The choice between psychotherapy and medication, or a combination of both, depends on the individual's specific diagnosis, symptom severity, and personal preferences. Healthcare providers work collaboratively with individuals to determine the most appropriate treatment plan.

It's worth noting that lifestyle modifications, stress management techniques, and support from friends and family can complement these treatment approaches. In the subsequent chapters, we will explore coping strategies and support systems that can enhance the management of anxiety disorders.

Describe the role of SSRIs (Selective Serotonin Reuptake Inhibitors)

Selective Serotonin Reuptake Inhibitors, commonly known as SSRIs, are a class of medications frequently prescribed in the treatment of anxiety disorders. These medications play a crucial role in alleviating anxiety symptoms and improving the overall well-being of individuals affected by these conditions.

How SSRIs Work

SSRIs primarily target the regulation of serotonin, a neurotransmitter in the brain associated with mood, emotions, and overall well-being. These medications work by blocking the reuptake of serotonin in the brain, allowing it to remain in the synaptic gap between neurons for a longer period. This, in turn, increases the availability of serotonin, which can have several positive effects on individuals with anxiety disorders:

Improved Mood: By enhancing serotonin levels, SSRIs can elevate mood and reduce the persistent feelings of sadness and anxiety associated with anxiety disorders.

Reduced Anxiety: SSRIs can help individuals manage the physical and mental symptoms of anxiety, such as rapid heartbeat, excessive worry, and restlessness.

Enhanced Resilience: These medications can improve the ability to cope with stress and anxiety-provoking situations.

Common SSRIs Used in Anxiety Disorder Treatment

Several SSRIs have been approved by healthcare authorities for the treatment of anxiety disorders. Some of the most commonly prescribed SSRIs include:

Sertraline (Zoloft): Sertraline is used to treat various anxiety disorders, including Generalized Anxiety Disorder (GAD), Social Anxiety Disorder, and Panic Disorder.

Escitalopram (Lexapro): Escitalopram is effective in the treatment of GAD and Social Anxiety Disorder.

Fluoxetine (Prozac): Fluoxetine can be prescribed for a range of anxiety disorders, including GAD, Social Anxiety Disorder, and Panic Disorder.

Paroxetine (Paxil): Paroxetine is often used in the treatment of Social Anxiety Disorder, Panic Disorder, and Obsessive-Compulsive Disorder (OCD).

Considerations and Side Effects

While SSRIs are generally considered safe and effective, it's essential for individuals and their healthcare providers to be aware of potential side effects and considerations. Common side effects can include nausea, headaches, and changes in sleep patterns. In some cases, SSRIs may take several weeks to reach their full therapeutic effect.

Moreover, individuals taking SSRIs should be monitored closely by their healthcare provider to ensure that the medication is providing the desired benefits and not causing adverse effects. Adjustments to the dosage or medication may be necessary in some cases.

SSRIs have been instrumental in improving the quality of life for countless individuals struggling with anxiety disorders. These medications, when used in conjunction with psychotherapy and lifestyle modifications, can provide a comprehensive approach to managing anxiety and regaining a sense of control and well-being. In the following chapters, we will delve into coping strategies and support systems that can further enhance the journey to recovery.

Chapter 7: Coping Strategies for Daily Life

Practical coping strategies for managing anxiety in everyday situations

Managing anxiety in everyday life is a crucial aspect of coping with anxiety disorders. While professional treatment plays a significant role, individuals can also employ practical coping strategies to navigate daily challenges and minimize the impact of anxiety. Here are some practical coping strategies to consider:

Deep Breathing: When anxiety strikes, practice deep breathing. Inhale slowly through your nose, allowing your abdomen to expand, and then exhale slowly through your mouth. Deep breaths can help calm your nervous system and reduce the intensity of anxiety symptoms.

Mindfulness Meditation: Mindfulness meditation involves focusing your attention on the present moment without judgment. Regular practice can help you become more aware of your thoughts and emotions, allowing you to respond to anxiety with greater resilience.

Progressive Muscle Relaxation: This technique involves systematically tensing and then relaxing different muscle groups in your body. It can help reduce physical tension and promote relaxation.

Time Management: Create a daily schedule or to-do list to help you stay organized and reduce the feeling of being overwhelmed. Prioritize tasks and break them into smaller, manageable steps.

Limit Stimulants: Reduce or eliminate stimulants like caffeine and nicotine from your diet. These substances can exacerbate anxiety symptoms.

Healthy Lifestyle Choices: Regular exercise, a balanced diet, and adequate sleep can significantly impact your overall well-being. Physical activity releases endorphins, which can enhance mood and reduce anxiety.

Social Support: Stay connected with friends and family. Talking to a trusted person about your feelings can provide emotional support and alleviate anxiety.

Avoid Alcohol and Recreational Drugs: Substance use can temporarily mask anxiety symptoms but often worsens them in the long run. Avoid or limit alcohol and recreational drugs.

Challenge Negative Thoughts: Use cognitive-behavioral techniques to challenge irrational or negative thoughts that fuel anxiety. Ask yourself if your worries are based on facts or assumptions.

Practice Gratitude: Keep a gratitude journal and write down things you're grateful for each day. Shifting your focus to positive aspects of life can reduce anxiety.

Engage in Relaxation Exercises: Activities like yoga, tai chi, or progressive muscle relaxation can help calm both the body and mind, reducing anxiety symptoms.

Limit News Consumption: Continuous exposure to distressing news can increase anxiety. Set boundaries on how much news you consume and consider credible sources.

Seek Professional Help: If anxiety is significantly impacting your life, don't hesitate to seek professional help. Therapy and medication can be highly effective in managing anxiety disorders.

Remember that coping strategies may vary from person to person. It's essential to find what works best for you and incorporate these strategies into your daily routine. Combining these practical coping methods with professional treatment can provide a comprehensive approach to managing anxiety and enhancing your overall well-being.

Discuss stress management techniques, deep breathing, and relaxation exercises

Effective stress management is a vital component of coping with anxiety disorders and maintaining overall well-being. Stress can exacerbate anxiety symptoms, so adopting stress-reduction techniques is essential. Here, we explore stress management techniques, deep breathing, and relaxation exercises:

Stress Management Techniques

Identify Stressors: Begin by identifying the sources of your stress. Recognizing what triggers your anxiety can help you take proactive steps to manage it.

Time Management: Organize your day and tasks. Create a schedule that allocates time for work, relaxation, and self-care.

Prioritize essential activities and avoid overloading your schedule.

Problem-Solving: When faced with a stressful situation, engage in problem-solving. Identify potential solutions and take steps to address the issue at hand.

Set Realistic Goals: Establish achievable goals and expectations for yourself. Unrealistic expectations can lead to unnecessary stress.

Physical Activity: Regular exercise is a powerful stress reducer. Physical activity releases endorphins, which are natural mood lifters.

Deep Breathing

Deep breathing is a simple yet effective relaxation technique that can be used to manage anxiety in the moment. Here's how to practice deep breathing:

Find a Quiet Space: Locate a quiet and comfortable place where you won't be disturbed.

Sit or Lie Down: Sit in a comfortable chair or lie down on your back. Close your eyes if it helps you focus.

Inhale Slowly: Take a slow, deep breath through your nose, allowing your abdomen to rise as you fill your lungs.

Exhale Slowly: Exhale slowly through your mouth, emptying your lungs completely.

Repeat: Continue this process, focusing on your breath. Inhale for a count of four, hold for a count of four, and exhale for a count of four. Gradually increase the count as you become more comfortable with the technique.

Deep breathing helps activate the body's relaxation response, reducing tension and promoting a sense of calm.

Relaxation Exercises

Relaxation exercises aim to calm both the mind and body, alleviating anxiety symptoms. Here are some relaxation exercises to consider:

Yoga: Yoga combines physical postures, breathing techniques, and meditation to enhance relaxation and reduce stress.

Progressive Muscle Relaxation: This exercise involves systematically tensing and relaxing different muscle groups. It can help reduce physical tension and promote relaxation.

Mindfulness Meditation: Mindfulness meditation encourages you to focus your attention on the present moment without judgment. It can help you become more aware of your thoughts and emotions, promoting emotional regulation.

Visualization: Visualization exercises involve imagining peaceful and calming scenes or scenarios. This can help shift your focus away from anxiety-inducing thoughts.

Guided Imagery: Guided imagery involves listening to recordings or scripts that guide you through relaxing mental journeys, such as a walk through a serene forest or a day at the beach.

Incorporating these stress management techniques, deep breathing, and relaxation exercises into your daily routine can significantly reduce anxiety and improve your overall well-being. Experiment with these techniques to find the ones that work best for you and make them a regular part of your self-care routine.

Chapter 8: Finding Support

The significance of support from friends, family, and support groups

Coping with anxiety disorders can be a challenging journey, but you don't have to navigate it alone. The support of friends, family, and participation in support groups can be instrumental in managing anxiety and promoting recovery.

Friends and Family Support

Emotional Support: Friends and family can provide essential emotional support. Having someone who listens, understands, and empathizes with your struggles can alleviate feelings of isolation and anxiety.

Reduced Stigma: The stigma often associated with mental health issues can be lessened through open and supportive conversations with loved ones. When friends and family offer their understanding, it can reduce the shame often felt by individuals with anxiety disorders.

Practical Assistance: Loved ones can assist in practical ways, such as helping with daily tasks during periods of heightened anxiety or attending medical appointments with you.

Encouragement: Friends and family can be a source of encouragement, reinforcing your progress and motivating you to seek treatment or engage in coping strategies.

Education: Involving friends and family in your journey can help educate them about anxiety disorders, fostering a better understanding of your experience.

Support Groups

Shared Experiences: Support groups bring together individuals who share similar challenges. Sharing experiences and hearing from others who have faced anxiety disorders can be empowering and comforting.

Peer Learning: In support groups, you can learn from the coping strategies and experiences of others. This peer knowledge can offer practical insights into managing anxiety.

Sense of Belonging: Support groups provide a sense of belonging and acceptance. You can connect with individuals who understand your struggles and offer nonjudgmental support.

Reduced Isolation: Anxiety disorders can often lead to feelings of isolation. Joining a support group helps counter this isolation and provides a network of people who genuinely care about your well-being.

Validation: Hearing others share their stories and challenges can validate your own experiences, helping you feel less alone in your journey.

Engaging with support networks not only eases the emotional burden of anxiety disorders but also provides practical assistance and encouragement. Whether through conversations with friends and family or participation in support groups, you'll find that sharing your experiences and receiving support from others can be a crucial component of your path to recovery.

Anxiety and Depression Association (ADAA)

Accessing reliable information and support is a vital aspect of managing anxiety disorders. Organizations like the Anxiety and Depression Association of America (ADAA) play a crucial role in providing resources, education, and a sense of community for individuals affected by anxiety disorders.

The Anxiety and Depression Association of America (ADAA)

The ADAA is a prominent nonprofit organization dedicated to promoting the prevention, treatment, and cure of anxiety, depression, and related disorders. Here's how the ADAA can be a valuable resource:

Education: The ADAA offers a wealth of educational resources, including articles, webinars, and publications, aimed at increasing awareness and understanding of anxiety disorders.

Support and Community: The organization provides a platform for individuals to connect with others who are dealing with anxiety. Through forums and online communities, you can share your experiences and find support.

Expert Insights: The ADAA connects individuals with mental health professionals and experts who can offer guidance and answers to questions about anxiety disorders.

Treatment Options: The organization provides information about various treatment options, including therapy and medication, to help individuals make informed decisions about their care.

Advocacy: The ADAA advocates for mental health awareness and access to quality care. By staying informed about their advocacy efforts, you can contribute to the larger conversation about mental health.

Events and Conferences: The ADAA hosts events and conferences that offer a chance to learn from leading experts and engage in discussions about anxiety disorders.

Online Screenings: The ADAA offers free and confidential online screenings for anxiety and mood disorders, which can be a helpful first step for individuals who are unsure about their symptoms.

By accessing resources provided by organizations like the ADAA, individuals can gain valuable insights, connect with others facing similar challenges, and find the support they need on their journey to managing anxiety disorders effectively. Remember that you're not alone in this process, and there are organizations like the ADAA dedicated to helping you lead a happier, healthier life.

Chapter 9: Anxiety in Recovery

Address anxiety during recovery from substance abuse and addiction

Recovery from substance abuse and addiction is a significant achievement, but it often comes with its unique challenges, including the experience of anxiety. It's essential to recognize and address anxiety during the recovery process.

Causes of Anxiety in Recovery

Post-Acute Withdrawal Symptoms (PAWS): Many individuals in early recovery experience PAWS, which can include symptoms such as anxiety, depression, insomnia, and cravings. These symptoms can be a result of the brain and body adjusting to life without substances.

Adjustment to Sobriety: The transition to a sober lifestyle can be anxiety-inducing. Coping with stressors without the use of substances can be challenging.

Coping Strategies in Recovery

Meditation and Mindfulness: Engaging in meditation and mindfulness practices can help individuals manage anxiety in recovery. These techniques promote self-awareness and emotional regulation.

Yoga and Exercise: Physical activity, such as yoga or regular exercise, can have a profound impact on mood and anxiety. It releases endorphins, which are natural mood enhancers.

Talk to a Friend or Sponsor: Sharing your feelings with a trusted friend, sponsor, or support group member can provide emotional support and alleviate anxiety.

Grounding Exercises: Grounding techniques involve techniques like focusing on your surroundings or using the 5-4-3-2-1 exercise, which can help reduce the intensity of anxiety symptoms.

Work the 12 Steps: Engaging in the 12-step recovery program can provide structure and support for individuals in recovery. The steps include processes for addressing anxiety and other emotional challenges.

Healthy Distractions: Engaging in activities you enjoy, such as hobbies or creative pursuits, can serve as healthy distractions from anxiety.

Professional Help: If anxiety significantly interferes with daily life or poses a risk of relapse, it may be necessary to seek professional help. Therapists and counselors can provide specialized guidance.

Addressing anxiety in recovery is essential for maintaining sobriety and overall well-being. By implementing these coping strategies and seeking support from peers and professionals, individuals can effectively manage anxiety and continue on the path to a fulfilling and substance-free life.

Post-acute withdrawal symptoms (PAWS) and strategies to manage anxiety

Recovery from substance abuse and addiction often involves confronting not only the initial withdrawal symptoms but also a set of challenges known as Post-Acute Withdrawal Symptoms (PAWS). These symptoms, including anxiety, can persist beyond the initial detoxification period. Understanding PAWS and implementing strategies to manage anxiety during this phase are essential for successful recovery.

PAWS refers to a cluster of protracted withdrawal symptoms that can occur after the initial detoxification phase. These symptoms are often associated with anxiety and can include:

Anxiety: Persistent feelings of unease, nervousness, and apprehension are common in PAWS.

Depression: Individuals in PAWS may experience persistent sadness and a lack of interest or pleasure in previously enjoyed activities.

Irritability: An increased irritability and difficulty in managing frustration and anger can be observed.

Cravings: Intense cravings for the substance of abuse may continue to be present.

Sleep Disturbances: Difficulty falling asleep or maintaining a regular sleep pattern is common.

Strategies to Manage Anxiety in PAWS

Mindfulness and Meditation*: Practices like mindfulness and meditation can help individuals become more aware of their thoughts and emotions and develop greater emotional regulation.

Stress Reduction Techniques: Engage in stress reduction techniques like progressive muscle relaxation, deep breathing exercises, or guided imagery to alleviate anxiety.

Healthy Lifestyle: Maintain a healthy lifestyle by incorporating regular exercise, a balanced diet, and adequate sleep into your routine. Physical activity, in particular, can release endorphins and reduce anxiety.

Peer Support: Connecting with peers who have experienced or are experiencing PAWS can provide a sense of community and understanding. Support groups can be invaluable.

Counseling and Therapy: Consider individual or group therapy to address the underlying issues contributing to anxiety and develop effective coping strategies.

Medication: In some cases, medication may be necessary to manage anxiety symptoms. Consult with a healthcare provider to determine the most appropriate treatment plan.

Self-Care: Prioritize self-care practices, including activities you enjoy and relaxation exercises. Self-care can be essential for managing anxiety during PAWS.

Structured Recovery Program: Engage in a structured recovery program, such as the 12-step model, to provide guidance and support during this challenging phase.

It's important to recognize that PAWS is a natural part of the recovery process. By addressing anxiety and other symptoms associated with PAWS through these strategies, individuals can navigate this phase more effectively and continue on the path to sustained recovery. Remember that with the right support and resources, anxiety during PAWS can be managed, and a fulfilling, substance-free life is attainable.

Chapter 10: A Brighter Future

Cultivating hope and resilience in dealing with anxiety disorders

Facing anxiety disorders can be a daunting journey, but it's essential to recognize that hope and resilience are powerful allies on the path to recovery. No matter how challenging the road may seem, there is always hope for a brighter, anxiety-free future.

The Power of Hope

Believe in Progress: Understand that recovery is a process, and progress may not always be linear. Celebrate even the smallest victories, as they are steps towards better mental health.

Seek Treatment: Recognize that professional help is available and can be highly effective in managing anxiety disorders. Reach out to therapists, counselors, and healthcare providers who specialize in treating these conditions.

Engage with Support Networks: Friends, family, and support groups offer valuable emotional support and a sense of community. Share your experiences and challenges with them, and allow them to be part of your journey.

Education and Awareness: Educate yourself about anxiety disorders and understand that they are treatable. Knowledge is a powerful tool in managing anxiety.

Building Resilience

Embrace Adaptability: Develop the ability to adapt to stressors and challenges. Resilience involves bouncing back from adversity and learning from difficult experiences.

Cultivate Coping Skills: Equip yourself with effective coping strategies, such as deep breathing, mindfulness, and stress management techniques. These skills can help you face anxiety head-on.

Set Realistic Goals: Establish achievable goals for your recovery journey. Progress may take time, but each step forward is a success.

Self-Compassion: Be kind to yourself and avoid self-criticism. Understand that setbacks are a natural part of recovery, and they do not define your worth or potential for healing.

Maintain a Healthy Lifestyle: Prioritize self-care by maintaining a balanced diet, regular exercise, and adequate sleep. Physical health plays a significant role in emotional well-being.

Professional Help: Don't hesitate to seek professional assistance when needed. Therapists, counselors, and healthcare providers can offer specialized guidance.

Stay Connected: Isolation can exacerbate anxiety. Keep connections with supportive individuals who understand and care about your well-being.

Remember that resilience is not about avoiding difficulties but about finding the strength to navigate them. Hope is the belief that better days are ahead, and resilience is the ability to endure the journey.

Your experiences, challenges, and triumphs can be a source of inspiration and support for others facing anxiety disorders. By cultivating hope and resilience, you not only improve your own well-being but also contribute to a community of understanding, compassion, and recovery. Together, we can strive for a future free from the burdens of anxiety, one filled with hope, resilience, and brighter tomorrows.

Key takeaways and a message of support

Key Takeaways

- Understanding anxiety disorders is crucial for individuals and their support networks. These disorders can impact daily life and well-being.

- Common anxiety disorders include Generalized Anxiety Disorder (GAD), Social Anxiety Disorder, and Panic Disorder.
- Anxiety disorders are influenced by a combination of genetic, environmental, and psychological factors.
- Physical and mental symptoms of anxiety disorders can vary, impacting both the body and mind.
- Diagnosis involves a comprehensive evaluation of symptoms, medical history, physical exams, and psychological assessments.
- Treatment options include psychotherapy, medication, or a combination of both.
- Coping strategies like stress management techniques, deep breathing, and relaxation exercises can help manage anxiety.

- Support from friends, family, and support groups is essential in the journey to recovery.
- Organizations like the Anxiety and Depression Association of America (ADAA) offer valuable resources and a sense of community.
- Anxiety can persist during recovery from substance abuse and addiction, and managing it is vital.
- Post-Acute Withdrawal Symptoms (PAWS) may include anxiety, and strategies like mindfulness and counseling can help manage these symptoms.
- Cultivating hope and resilience is essential. Recovery is a process, and there is always hope for a brighter, anxiety-free future.

Message of Support

If you are facing anxiety disorders, know that you are not alone on this journey. There is hope, there are resources, and there is support available to help you manage and overcome anxiety. Your experiences, challenges, and triumphs can inspire others and create a community of understanding and compassion.

Recovery is a process, and progress may not always be linear, but every step forward is a success. Reach out to friends, family, and support groups. Seek professional help when needed. Embrace hope and resilience as your allies.

You have the strength to navigate anxiety and emerge from it with greater understanding, resilience, and well-being. Your journey is a testament to your courage, and there are brighter days ahead.

Conclusion

In conclusion, this book has explored the multifaceted world of anxiety disorders and provided a comprehensive understanding of their causes, symptoms, diagnosis, and treatment options. It has emphasized the importance of support from friends, family, and support groups in the journey to recovery and highlighted the significant role of organizations like the Anxiety and Depression Association of America (ADAA) in providing resources and community.

The book has also addressed the unique challenges of managing anxiety during recovery from substance abuse and addiction, shedding light on the impact of Post-Acute Withdrawal Symptoms (PAWS) and strategies to manage them effectively.

Ultimately, this book carries a message of hope and resilience. It reminds readers that recovery is a process, progress may not always be linear, but there is always hope for a brighter, anxiety-free future. By understanding, addressing, and learning to manage anxiety disorders, individuals can embark on a path toward better mental health and well-being.

Remember, you are not alone in this journey, and there is support available. Each step forward, no matter how small, is a success, and brighter days are ahead. Cultivate hope, embrace resilience, and know that you have the strength to navigate anxiety and emerge from it with a deeper understanding of yourself and a brighter future.

www.ingramcontent.com/pod-product-compliance
Lightning Source LLC
Chambersburg PA
CBHW070910260726
48661CB00004B/1685